Circus: Handicap Haikus

Ananda Rose Bennett

All works are original creations by Ananda Rose Bennett
© 2020 by the author
All Rights Reserved

Published by Doctor's Dreams Publishing
PO Box 4808
Biloxi, MS 39535, USA
writerpllevin@gmail.com

No part of this production may be reproduced, stored in a retrieval system, or transmitted in any form or by any means, electronic, mechanical, recording, or otherwise, without the prior written permission of the author.

All characters, situations, and locations are fictional unless otherwise specified. Any resemblance to people real or past is purely coincidental.

Prepared and published in the United States of America

ICBN: 978-1-942181-19-4

Acknowledgments:
Special thanks to Philip Levin, MD, for his editing, graphic construction, and publishing.
Cover Illustration by Molly Chopin
Assistance with writing and editing by Cassandra J. Perry
Photography by Dark Chamber Photography.

Dedication

To Ryan, for inspiring me to start writing again. To my mama, for always taking care of me. To Lauren, for being a best friend for life. To Philip, for saying "Yes" to this book. And to Sean, for loving me, no matter how annoying I get.

Table of Contents

Chapter 1   Quad Life

Chapter 2   Monkey Man

Chapter 3   By Others

Chapter 4   Nursing

Chapter 5   Technology

Chapter 6   Weed

Chapter 7   Ridiculousness

Chapter 8   Sex

Chapter 9   Poly

Chapter 10   Camming

Chapter 11   Politics

Chapter 12   Life Stories

Chapter One: Quad Life

I've been a quadriplegic for twenty years. After two decades, you can get used to anything. I am not only used to my quad life, but I'm pretty happy with it. It was very difficult in the beginning and still can be a little difficult. But having a good perspective on the situation can make a huge difference. That's why I try to always make fun of my situation. Laughter really is the best medicine even if it's only a deflection on my part. Mental health is also important to keep the monsters at bay; I rely on my Zoloft and regular therapy appointments.

I also like to remember that my life could be a whole lot worse. By thinking about others who might not have the luxuries that I do it helps me realize how very fortunate I am to be alive and to be loved. I consider myself a very lucky woman to have become the person I am today, and for being able to live the life that I do. Life is way too much fun to let an unfortunate situation keep me from living it.

.

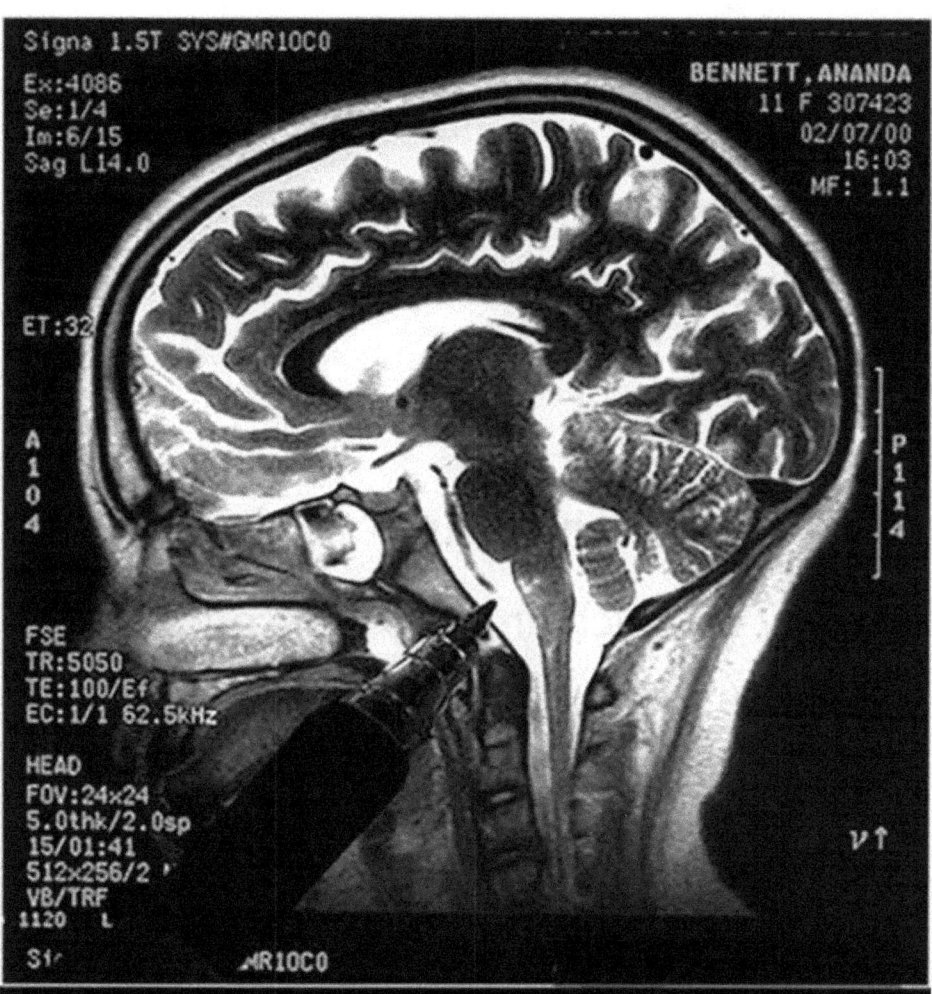

Dr.   points out the region of   brain that indicates a stroke in her brain stem. The stoke paralyzed her from the neck down.

Quad Life

Wheelchairs aren't so bad.

My wheelchair gives me freedom.

My wheelchair is rad!

Quad Life

Spasms are the worst

I shake but I don't shiver.

Don't let me kick you.

Quad Life

Every half hour

Computer says, "Drink bitch drink!"

I will sip and gulp

Quad Life

I drank all day long

Hurry babe, I gotta pee bad!

Yay, my kidneys work!

Quad Life

Listen you asshole!

You need to start working right.

I'm tired of your shit.

Quad Life

I pee in haikus
Five seventy five *CC*'s
My urine is Zen

Chapter Two: Monkey Man

Sean takes care of me because he loves me. Even before he met me, I told him, "You'll have to learn how to take care of me before we can be alone." His response was a simple, "Okay." After three weeks of emails and phone calls, we had our first date. Even though it was simple, it was the most amazing date I've ever been on. He came over to my house where I was living with my mom, dad, my older sister, and my nephew. He fed me coconut shrimp fresh out of the microwave with mango salsa. We watched two of my favorite movies, "Snatch" and "Natural Born Killers." Afterwards I gave him the "get over here" head motion and told him I wanted him to kiss me. We've been together ever since. Sean is the sweetest man I've ever met, and without him I would be lost.

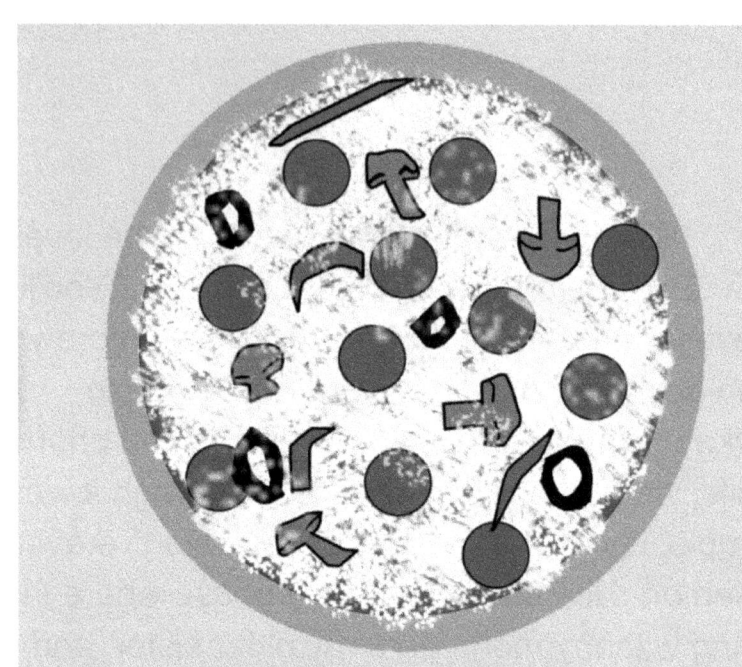

Monkey Man

Monkey Man eat now!

Chairwoman, order pizza!

Monkey Man happy

Monkey Man

What's that awful smell?

It's those damn dirty dishes

I hate washing them!

Monkey Man

Damn you Domino's!

Why must you send me promos?

You make life harder!

Chapter Three: By Others

A huge part of what makes my life so awesome is the people in it. I have an amazing support system of family, friends, and caretakers. They enrich and contribute to my life more than I could ever repay them for. I may never be able to be alone for more than two minutes at a time for the rest of my life, but the ends justify the means.

My "Quad Squad" influences every aspect of my life. It was inevitable that I would include them in this book.

By Others

My legs are crippled

I have a warrior's heart

I ask, "Who needs legs?"

By Others

Your butt's a haiku

I like to slap it a lot

It's my favorite butt

By Others

I don't date dumb whores

Girls who don't like haikus suck.

Go fist your own butt!

By Others

Feeling impatient?
Take a moment and just breathe
Meditate a bit

By Others

Friction is my friend

That is not always the case

Only when mopping

By Others

Weird, womanly, quad.
Her haiku skill often awed.
Stand up, let's applaud!

By Others

Banana bunnies

Some governors don't like them.

They are my hunnies

By Others

I am paralyzed

Just a faulty blood vessel

Left me in this chair

By Others

When faced with illness

Some surrender to cruel fate

Others strive and thrive.

Chapter Four: Nursing

One of the many realities of being a high level quad[1] is that I am never alone. Not only have I grown used to that, but I am very grateful for it. Some people tell me that, for them, never being alone would be the hardest part of living my life.

I receive up to 16 hours of in-home nursing care on most days. This means nurses come to my apartment and take care of me. I absolutely love every minute they're here because my nurses get me out of bed in the morning, put me back in bed at night, and pretty much everything in between. My nurses help me live my life. But not everything is kittens and glitter.

The downside of home health is that sometimes I have to work with a nurse who I really don't like or get along with. But I can put up with a religious know it all if she never calls out, is punctual, and she takes excellent care of me. I have also dealt with the opposite of this situation and I honestly cannot tell you which is worse.

---

[1] Someone with a high injury level. Generally, the higher the injury level the less movement and independence a quadriplegic will have.

Sometimes you'll meet a nurse that just gets you: they share your beliefs and your sense of humor, they're open-minded and they appreciate your kind of crazy, and to top it off, they're a great nurse. Those nurses are hard to find so when you do get one of those nurses, make damn sure they know how much you appreciate them and everything they do for you.

Over time, these incredible nurses can become great friends... but wait for the other shoe to drop because eventually one of your nurses that you thought was like family will quit while your primary nurse is on vacation, leaving your boyfriend to take care of you for 24-hours a day for a solid week. Don't forget, people are assholes!

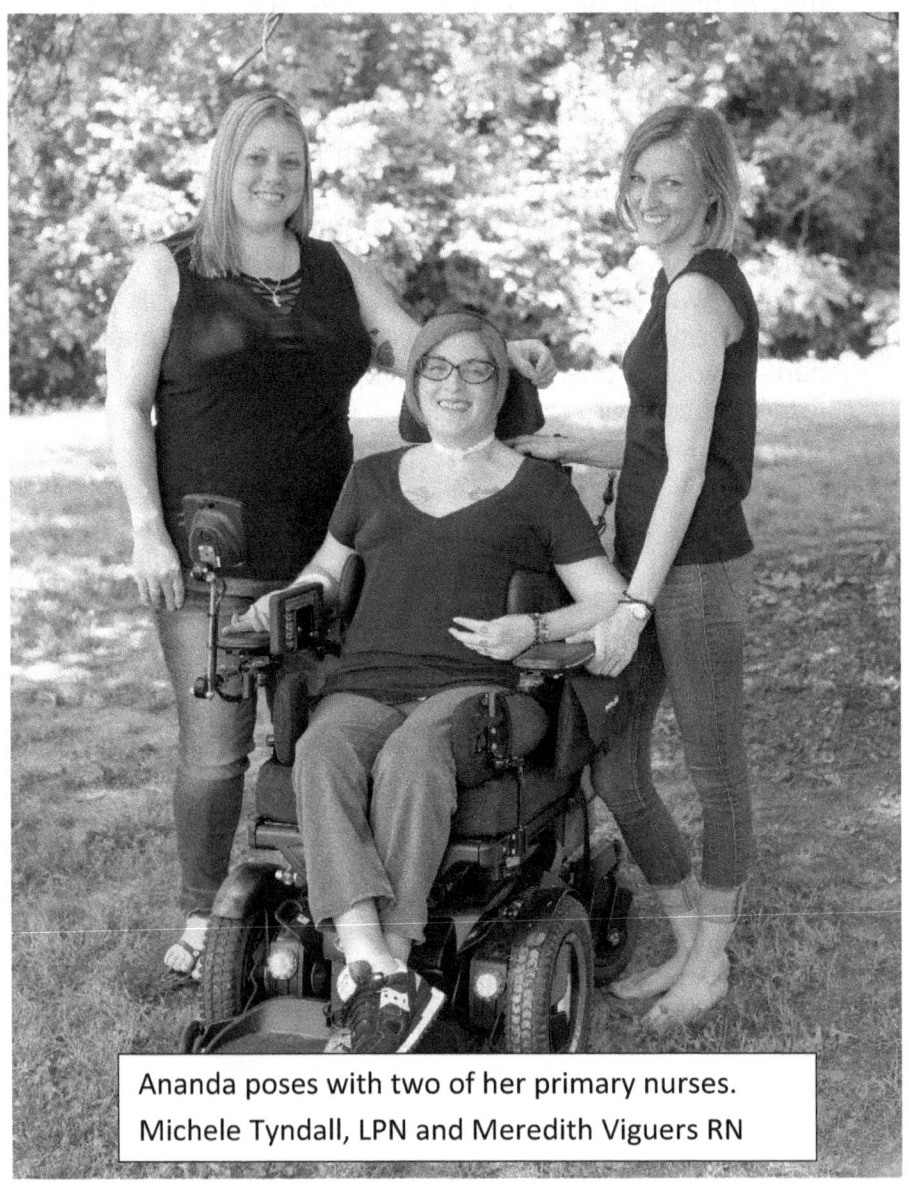

Ananda poses with two of her primary nurses. Michele Tyndall, LPN and Meredith Viguers RN

Nursing

Check me rectally

Would you please change your gloves now?

Same time tomorrow.

Nursing

Mer tall bird woman

Do NOT fall short on the job.

She'll come after you

Nursing

Lighting is vital.

For shaving a quad's pussy

Home health nurses rock!

Chapter Five: Technology

    The year 2000 was an amazing year to have a stroke because technology was booming and as a result of that my life was saved. If ventilators hadn't been invented I wouldn't be here today. I was completely ventilator-dependent for a little more than three months. Now I only use one at night. My entire life revolves around technology as I'm sure the majority of your lives do, too. But it's a little different for me.

    The technologies that I love the most are the ones that give me a small sense of independence. One very important example is my wheelchair. Without my power wheelchair, its chin joystick, and its Bluetooth connectivity, I wouldn't be able to navigate my environment the way I want to. What that really means is I can swerve when I want, I can speed up when I want, I can leave the room when I'm pissed off, and a million other things that let me control something in my life. If I couldn't control where and when my wheelchair moved, I would be one very depressed quad.

    My wheelchair does so much more than move me from place to place. It turns my chin joystick into a Bluetooth mouse. It enables me to use my computer in ways that I never knew

I would need to or be able to do. With my computer software, I can type, click, and double click like everyone else. But what that really means is that I could write papers in college, I can manage a bank account, I can join a dating site, I can reach out to the community around me, I can write a book, and so much more.

Another one of my most favorite technological advancements from the past few years is the QuadStick. The QuadStick is a mouth-operated video game controller made for quadriplegics that works on all major consoles as well as PCs, and Macs. After my old adaptive controller broke 10 years ago, being able to play video games again is a wonderful gift and I am extremely grateful for it. But the most amazing activity that the QuadStick enables me to do is create art. I've been able to paint digitally with my chin joystick but the QuadStick gives me the fluid movement that I didn't know I was missing. Now, for the first time in 19 years, I am happy with the work that I'm producing.

Technology has advanced so much and so fast since the year 2000. For my entire "quad life" I've been dreaming about environmental controls that would let me manipulate lamps and other electronics with my voice. Today, not only do they exist, they are commercialized for $50! I can't wait to see what new technology the next decade brings!

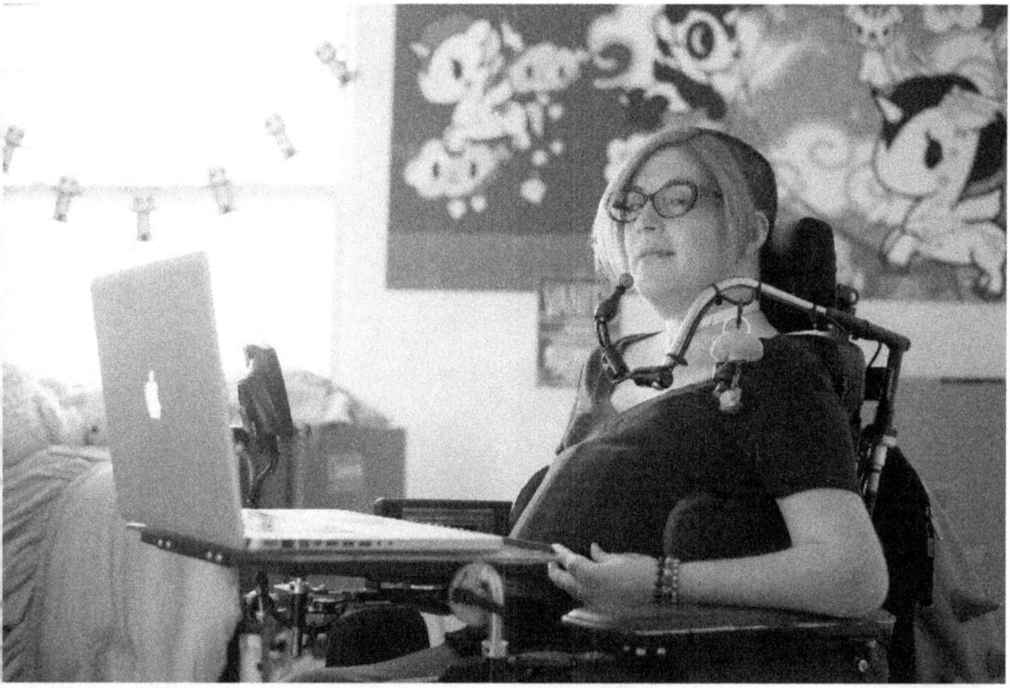

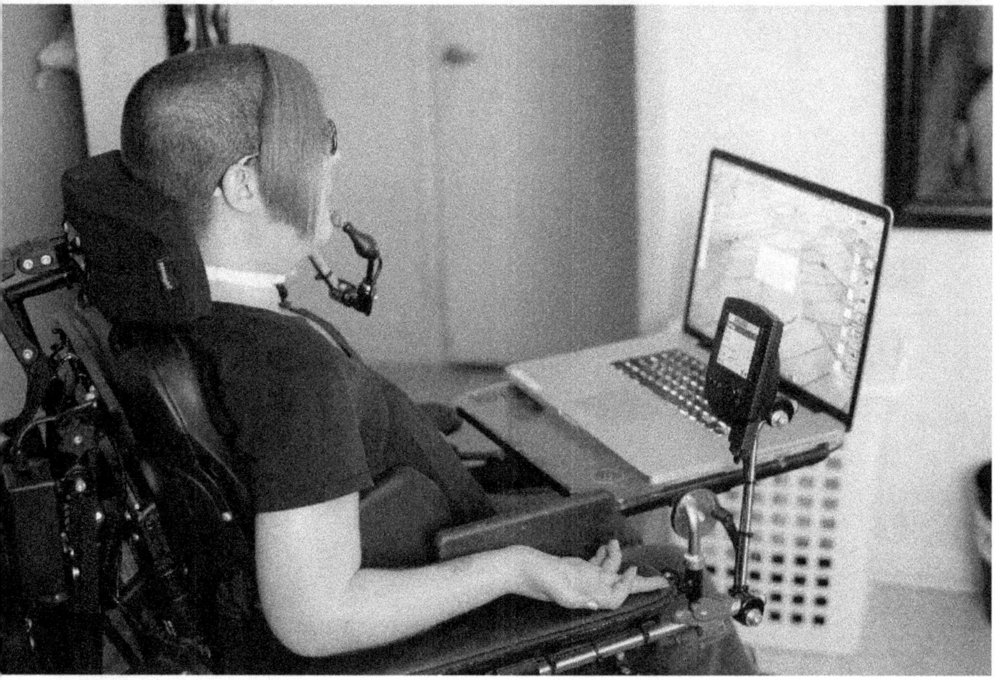

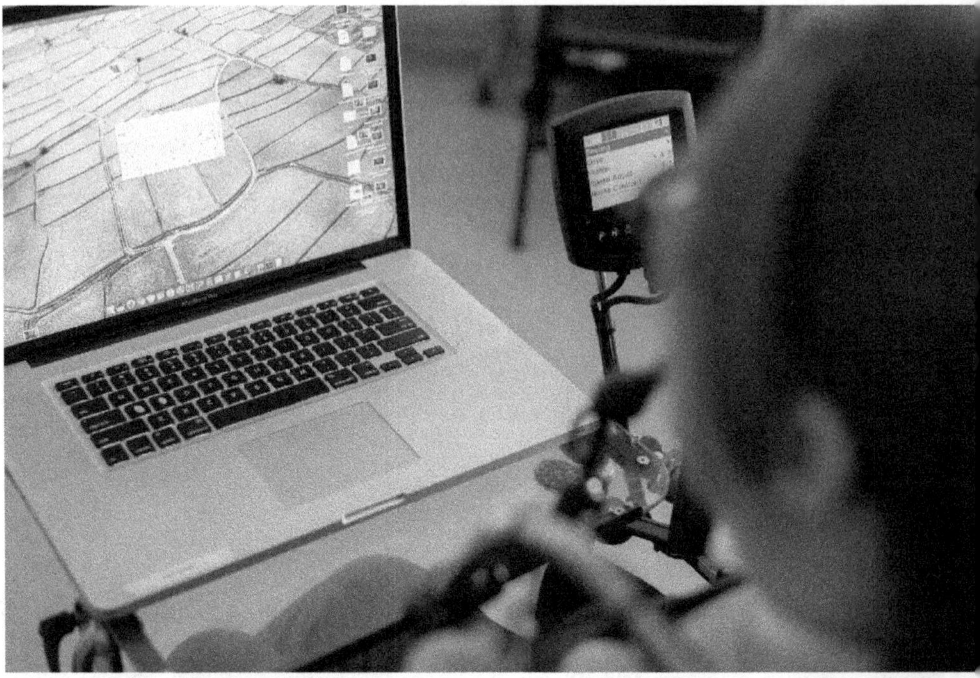

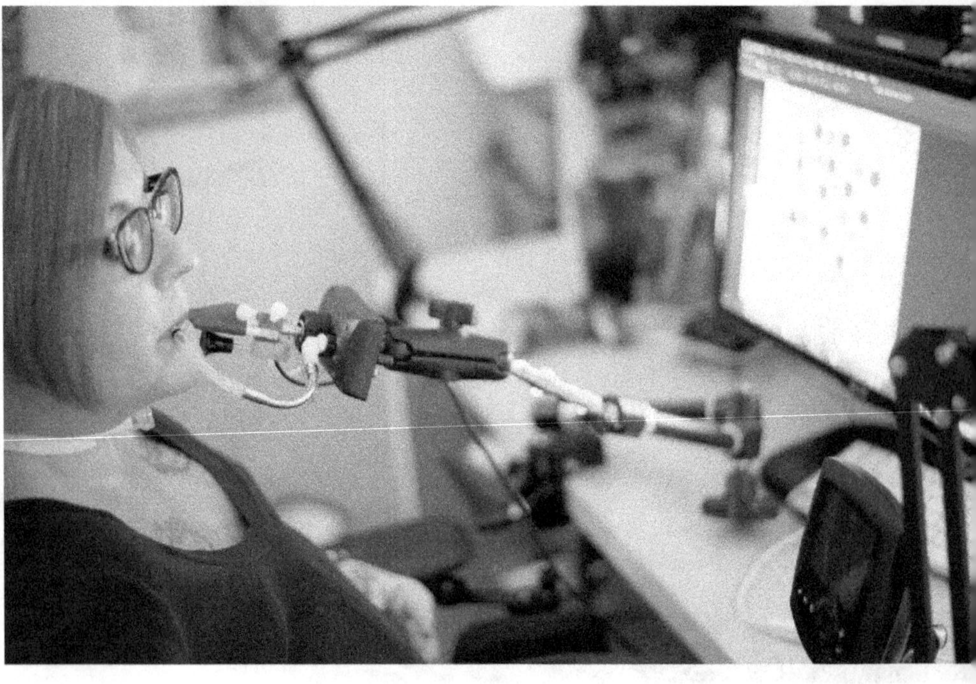

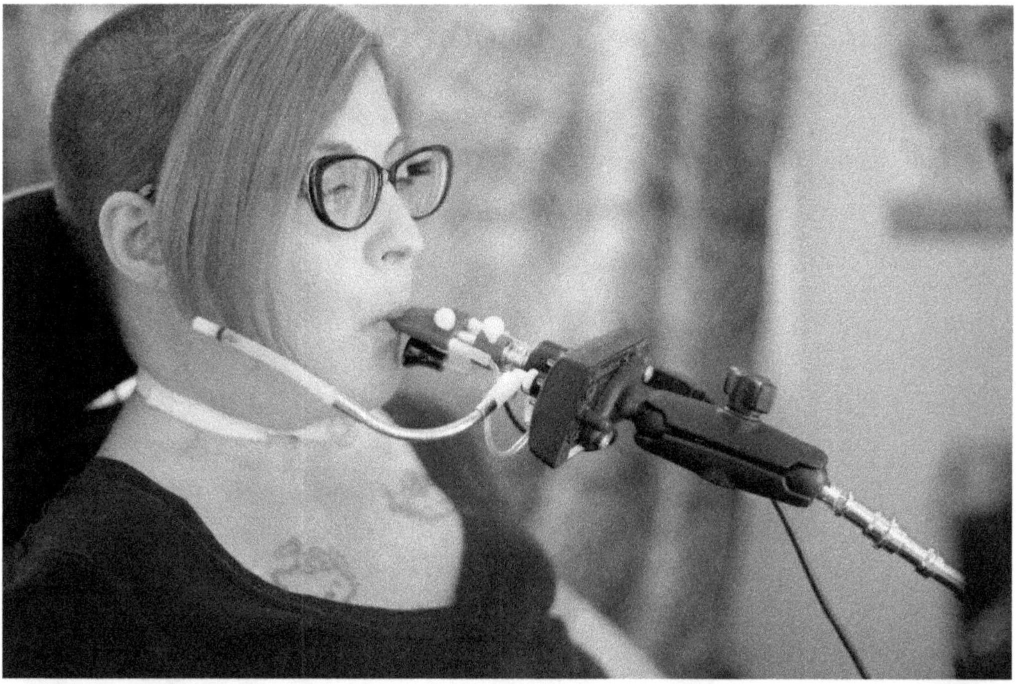

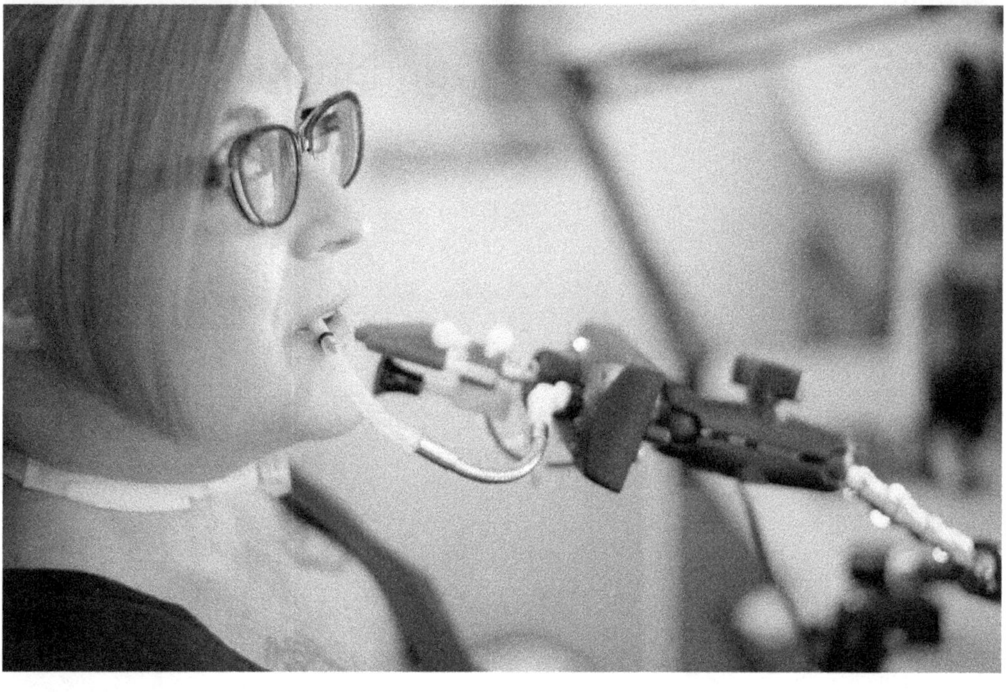

Technology

An important tool

Without it my art is shit

I love the QuadStick!

Technology

Speech recognition

It can save you lots of time

But training is a bitch

Technology

Need a good doorstop?

Then use your PlayStation 2

They are obsolete

Technology

Oh beach ball of death!

You make me so unhappy.

Please go away now.

Technology

My Passy-Muir Valve

The best invention ever

Hear me speak, bitches!

Technology

The little plumber

Sometimes he's a trash panda

He's a shapeshifter

Chapter Six: Weed

Salad, Ganja, Wacky Tobacky, it goes by many names. Marijuana has been a recreational drug for centuries, but its social acceptance and popularity is higher than ever today. This is because of the remarkable scientific breakthroughs we've delved into as a country with medical marijuana research. In 2017 marijuana shrinks cancer, it treats depression, anxiety, helps with glaucoma, and can aid many other ailments. If there ever was a super plant, marijuana would be it.

Aside from its ability to get me high, one of my favorite things about marijuana is how it relates to me. For those of you who don't know, my first name Ananda (Uh-non-duh) is a Hindi word that means bliss: the ultimate state of happiness. Many a temple, yoga studio, and spiritual movement, has been named and dedicated to the idea of Ananda. Reaching that state of bliss can sometimes be a challenge but one surefire way for me to achieve that state is by using marijuana. THC is so good at inducing the state of bliss that it mimics the effects of the naturally occurring neurotransmitter in our brain, known as "Anandamide" for its blissful effects. When I read that I thought "I was destined to be a pothead! Thanks, mama!"

For most of my adolescence, I knew that my entire immediate family were potheads. At the age of 16, I was eager to join in on the fun, but no one would help me get high. With me being underage I could understand their hesitation. But once I turned 18, they had no excuse. Yet no one wanted to be the first person to help me do what I had every right to do as a human being, just not the ability to do as a quad. But I was not giving up. So I took to the internet.

I'll never forget that day. Thomas came over with his bright blue mohawk and his globe vaporizer. He put it on the floor of my bedroom, plugged it in, and we talked while the glass globe began to fill with smoke. He was so cute and sweet. He sat beside me and helped me take hits from the plastic tube that was connected to the vape.

I know we were high as hell when my mom came in my room to tell me that my big sister Des had had a bad reaction to her new psych meds and had started hallucinating at work so she had called the ambulance. She was now at the ER, was feeling better, and should be home soon. I remember as soon as she closed the door I looked at Thomas and said, "Wow, what a buzzkill." Thomas laughed, smiled, and put the vaporizer's straw back in my mouth.

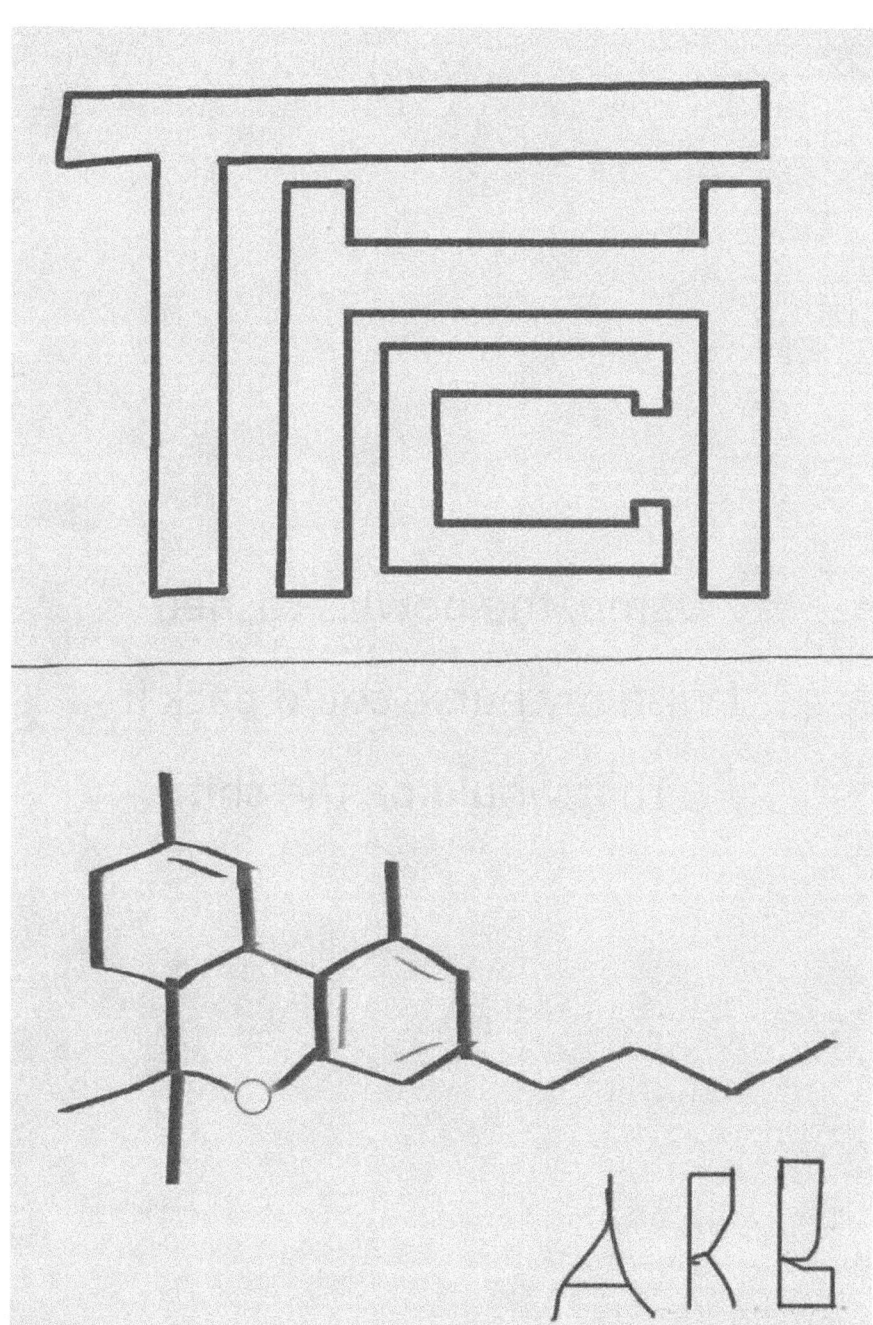

Weed

Damn, the bowl is cashed

I wish my nurse could pack it

That would be the shit

Weed

I have a headache

Would you please pack the bowl now?

That is delightful

Weed

Oh captain phuzzy!
Why do you make me wait here?
I want phuzzy now!

Weed

Chill the fuck out girl

The good things are worth the wait

Damn drug dealer time

Weed

My house smells like weed
People think something is wrong
When it doesn't reek

Chapter Seven: Ridiculousness

If someone were to describe me and my life to you it would sound like an absurd joke. It couldn't be written. It's too risqué and over the top but that is how I roll. Risqué and over the top are my preferred methods of everything. The funnier, the louder, the more colorful, the harder it is to believe, the more in your face and controversial something is, the better.

To some people, my life seems unbearable. But it's all about perspective in my opinion. I try to focus on the absurdity of a situation at every given moment and bring as much attention to it as possible by making fun of it. The joke may not make any sense. It may fail miserably or I'll hit it out of the park. Either way, it distracts me from whatever unpleasant thing is going on or it's celebrating something I'm enjoying and enhances it.

I try not to take myself too seriously and I always try to remember how long it took me to become who I am today, as well as how long it took me to be okay with who I am. I would say that a lot of my jokes end up with me being the butt of them. I love that and it makes me very happy because I feel that many people don't make fun of themselves enough. If you can't laugh at yourself, how are you going to handle what other people and the rest of the world might say about or to you? I get a lot of joy out of people making fun of me as long as I know their heart is in the right place.

I am very much a hedonist in that I believe everything you do in life should provide you with (or will eventually lead to) happiness and pleasure. I like things to never be boring; to be fun and exciting, loud and funny, and at most times, a little ridiculous. If you're doing something and it doesn't provide you with any type of joy or pleasure, my question to you is why the hell are you doing it?!

Ridiculousness

A prolapsed butthole

Is a sure way to ruin

A dinner party

Ridiculousness

Garlic jizz is yum

It's really just dipping sauce

But that's not funny!

Ridiculousness

Quad quad quad quad gimp

Gimpady gimpady gimp

Where's the cripple fight?!

Ridiculousness

Take melon. Leave sprout.

Now do the Hokey Pokey

Damn fool, you can dance!

Ridiculousness

Hobo taint sweat smell

I don't like that awful smell

Hobo wash your taint!

Chapter Eight: Sex

Sex is one of my biggest passions. It means a lot to me for more reasons than you might think. It's not only empowering, but also healing. The love and affection that I receive from my partner or partners can have a tremendous impact on my mental health. Once I learned that I was desired, even if most of it was sexual, I became confident. I became stronger knowing that I had the power and the choice to express myself sexually.

It has been through sex that I have gained my self-confidence. Sex has taught me that I am not alone and I don't have to be alone. Sex has taught me that I have another skill set and it has shown me that there is a niche market for myself.

Sex

One of the biggest reasons sex is important to me is because there is a huge misconception that individuals in wheelchairs can't have sex. It's often assumed, "You're in a wheelchair. You must not be able to have sex." Yes, it may be true for some but it isn't true for everyone. That's why every day I try to advocate for the rights of the disabled to have sex however they want and with whomever they want. *We have a right to orgasm and to make others orgasm just like everyone else.* That's why I choose to express myself sexually; not only because it feels good, but because I think the world needs to see it.

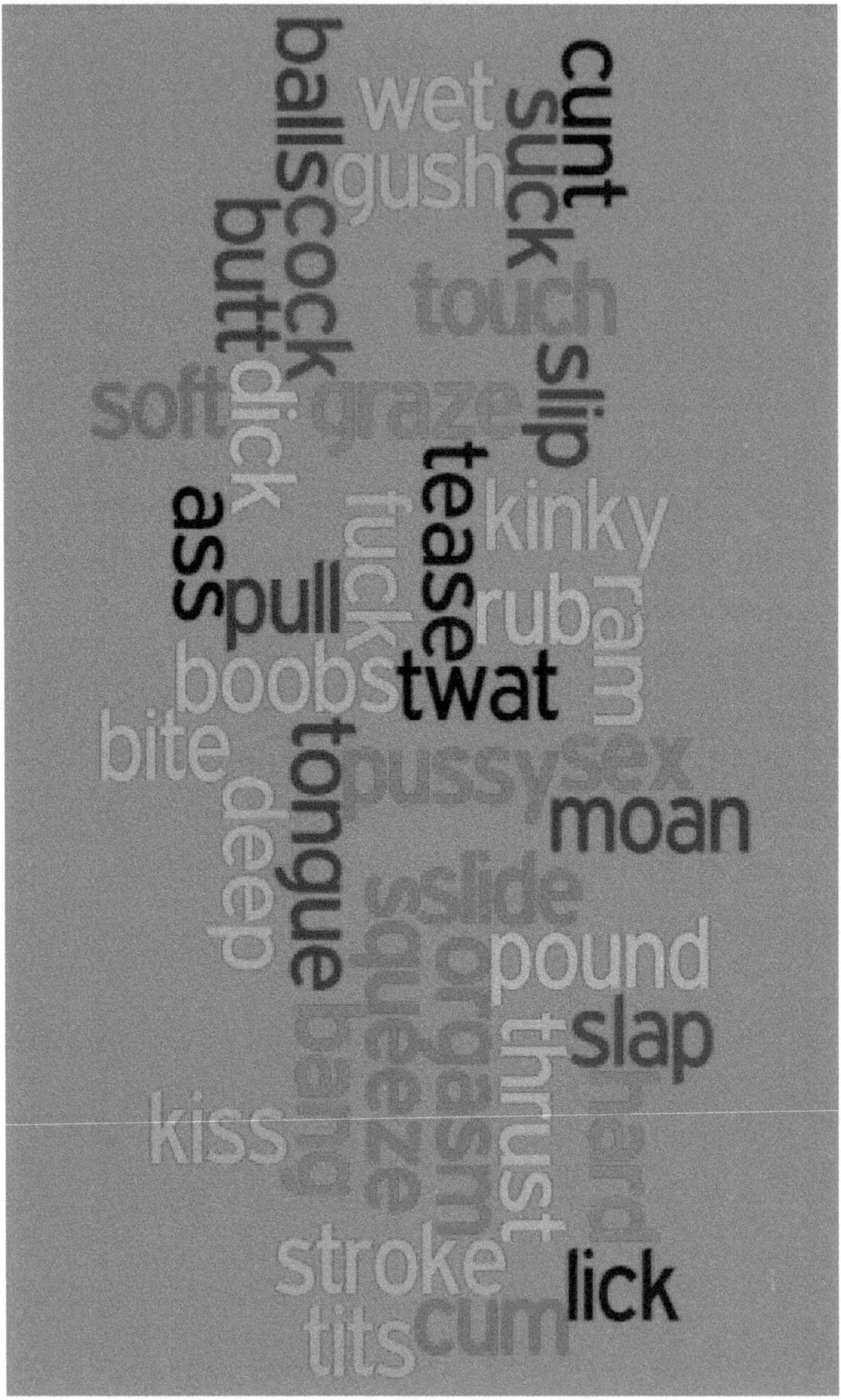
cunt
suck
wet
balls
gush
butt
cock
touch
slip
soft
dick
graze
tease
kinky
ass
pull
fuck
rub
ram
boobs
twat
bite
tongue
pussy
sex
moan
deep
slide
squeeze
orgasm
pound
slap
bang
thrust
hard
kiss
stroke
lick
tits
cum

Sex

As I just lay here

And you slide your cock in me

I will cum for you.

Sex

Face fuck me please Sir!

I love your cock in my throat

It feels so damn good.

Sex

I'm a naughty girl

Does that make me a good girl?

Sir says, "Yes it does."

Sex

Pussy is all wet

That is when it is the best

Nom nom nom nom nom

Sex

Sorry. Had to pee.

Thank you for understanding

Okay, let us fuck!

Sex

Sit the fuck down now.

You're a naughty little slut.

I'll tell you what's next.

Chapter Nine: Poly

After growing up listening to my parents argue, lie, and poorly communicate with each other, I already knew that the kind of relationship I wanted was an honest one. When I first started dating at the age of eighteen I dated for about a year and a half and during that time I met a lot of people who further emphasized my need for honesty and the ability to communicate. It was then that I was also introduced to polyamory, which I did not understand. I just thought polyamory was an excuse people used to try to sleep with everyone.

For those of you who don't know, "Poly," is short for Polyamory (from Greek πολύ poly, "many, several", and Latin amor, "love") which is the practice of, or desire for, intimate relationships with more than one partner, with the consent of all partners involved. It has been described as "consensual, ethical, and responsible non-monogamy".

I have been poly for almost a decade now and when I think about the journey that led me here, I realize how far I've come as well as how much my ideas on certain things have changed. When I was 18, I was monogamous, waiting for my prince charming to take my virginity when we made love on our wedding night. I wasn't confident or secure in who I was as a person. I thought "poly" was just a way to have your cake and eat it, too. But the life I have lived has changed my beliefs and my views. The poly lifestyle supports all of my needs and doesn't have a problem with how I've changed. I can't imagine going back to monogamy.

It wasn't until I wanted to explore my bi-curiosity further that Sean and I began to delve more into the poly lifestyle. I was in a committed monogamous relationship of five years with Sean. Early in our relationship I had mentioned my attraction to women, and like a lot of men, Sean was intrigued by my confession and that is where we started. I told him that I didn't just want to have sex with a woman but I would rather date a woman and have a relationship with her. But I had never kissed a woman and that was becoming increasingly frustrating for me.

I knew I was attracted to women since I was nine years old. I had been flirting with them for years, I almost exclusively watched all-lesbian porn, and Sean had seen me staring at beautiful women in public many more times than I had ever seen him checking out other women. But I needed to know for myself whether or not I was physically attracted to women to be able to say I truly knew who I was. Once we learned that a big part of polyamory was open and honest communication it almost seemed like a no-brainer because we had already been practicing open and honest communication for the past five years. So, we opened our relationship. As I began to explore my sexuality by way of dating and loving cis women and female identifying persons, I knew for sure that I was attracted to all genders, and this only increased my affinity and appreciation of the idea of having multiple partners.

After Sean and I first opened our relationship, like many poly couples we were trying to find a unicorn (a single bi or pansexual female) to complete that long-awaited fantasy of "trinogomy". But after waiting many months to find that pretty pony, you learn that they are as difficult to find as their moniker suggests. Initially I wasn't interested in dating other men. It wasn't because Sean and I had enacted a one-penis policy, either. I just had no interest in other men, or so I thought. But I wasn't having any more luck with the ladies on my own than I was when we pursued them as a couple. At that point we agreed as a couple that we would see other people and I would be free to see someone regardless of their gender.

Over the past few years Sean has had a girlfriend and I have had a few boyfriends, all of which have fizzled out or ended in heartbreak. Because we were emotionally bruised from failed friendships and relationships, we decided to take a break, not necessarily from seeing other people but from actively trying to pursue other partners. Throughout our entire almost decade long journey of being a poly couple, up until very recently we had never had a partner that was interested in both of us. That changed last year when a beautiful unicorn found us and it's been as magical as we thought it would be.

Some of those magical moments are that I now get to flirt with another person which means blowing twice as many kisses, sending more fun and sexy texts, and asking for my butt to be poked twice as often. I also love kissing one of my partners and telling them to "pass it on" to the other one. Sean and I have always enjoyed watching movies together but now we get to snuggle with our Sweet Bean as a throuple and enjoy those moments elevated with her in the middle (we alternate). We also have started gaming together! Playing video, card, and board games together is a whole lot of fun! Katelyn feels the extra comfort and support we provide her as well; for example, when she came out to her family we were there every step of the way regardless of how they might react.

    Sean and I always try to make sure Katelyn takes her meds before she gets too sleepy and I always make sure she has eaten. She says that we give her a space to vent, to get things off of her chest so she doesn't explode at random while at work. She also says that we let her live out her casual domesticity dreams of taking Sean to the grocery store, doing dishes, cleaning, and coming home to us some days after work. We also encourage her to come over when she's depressed and provide her with a constant stream of physical and emotional affection, for example we always tell her goodnight regardless of whether we are in the same room, we blow her kisses a lot, and tell her how smart and pretty she is.

    I'm so thankful for these wonderful people in my life. They give me the love, security, and emotional support that I dreamed about for so many years.

    For a very long time I didn't think someone as disabled as myself would find one long term partner let alone two! When I tell other disabled people about my partners they always tell me how incredible it is that I have them. I know having a loving partner and caregiver is something to be very grateful for. I feel like the luckiest quad in the world to have two awesome and loving partners.

    The idea of having a relationship with multiple partners is popular among the disabled community due to the appealing characteristic of sharing responsibilities and caregiving. The act of sharing responsibilities is so appealing in a relationship where one partner is disabled because so many of the physical responsibilities of a relationship fall onto the able-bodied partner. For example, Sean is responsible for taking care of me when I don't have a nurse and for doing things that are only possible when I do have a nurse, like going to the grocery store, paying rent, and picking up my medicine. But he also makes dinner for us, feeds me, helps me pee, helps me drink water every thirty minutes, and so much more. All of these small things add up to a lot of responsibilities over time.

    As much as I would like to say that I am not a burden on other people, it simply isn't true. I require a lot of care and attention. This can definitely be too much for one person to handle. That isn't anyone's fault and I am not complaining. I am just being honest and realistic with myself. But with another partner for us to love, to help do the things I can't, to help take care of me, and for us to take care of them by providing emotional support, it certainly can make life a little easier and sweeter.

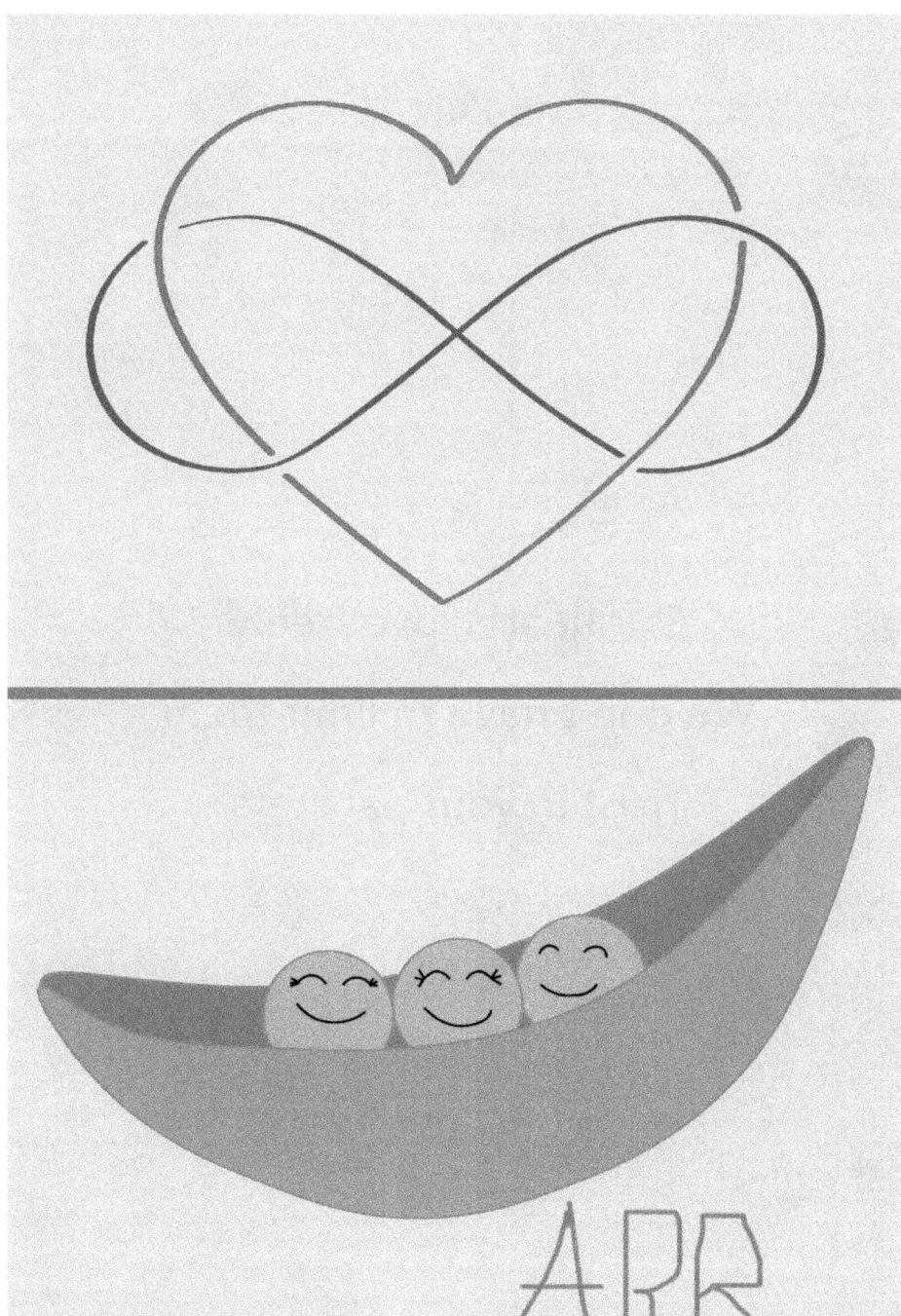

Poly

Our hearts love freely

We don't have to limit them

Trust in your partners

Poly

Cheaters lack the strength

To be polyamorous.

They are true cowards.

Poly

You, me, them, and her

We need to talk about that.

I'm so glad we did

Poly

Hello lovely bean

We miss you so much it hurts

We belong with you

Chapter Ten: Camming

Around 2015, I discovered how to masturbate with my mind. I call it my superpower. When I started camming in 2016, although I already knew that I was a voyeur and an exhibitionist, I had no idea how much I would enjoy camming nor how much it would help me. It helped me become more confident in my own body. I also found my audience.

I have fans all over the world that I get to talk to about all kinds of things, and they support what I do completely. They give me something to look forward to doing that has the potential to support me financially. I'm not only having a ton of fun, but I am educating people as well. I change the way people think about disability and sex. I know I harp on this a lot, but people are stupid. I once had a guy write to me in response to my cam partner ad saying he was interested but admitted later on that he was afraid that because I couldn't move he would feel like I wasn't giving consent and he didn't think he could "do that". After admitting that he felt that way, he also admitted to being an idiot for writing me in the first place.

So, when I seem enthusiastic about disability and sex there's a big fucking reason! Literally. With camming, I feel like I broaden the minds of all of those that see me and/or everyone I talk to.

Camming

You must send tokens

If you want to see my boobs

Keep the tip jar full

Camming

What they say is true

I have seen a lot of dick

Maybe just one more

Camming

Welcome to my room

Will you make me cum tonight?

I really hope so

Camming

A viewer once said

Is this where you want to be

When Jesus comes back?

Chapter Eleven: Politics

I don't even know where to start. Initially, I thought about stating the controversies of each of the presidents that have held office in my lifetime. But as I started to think about Bill Clinton's Oval Office blowjob, when he lied under oath during his impeachment trial; then George "Dubya" Bush stealing the election in 2000; September 11th; the war in Iraq; Weapons of Mass Destruction; and the recession I came to the same realization that I have come to several other times when trying to write this essay: that nothing that happened in politics from 2000 to 2016 was as bad as what is going on right now.

Our 45th President is a lying, cheating, affluent, manipulative, unintelligent, disrespectful, racist coward who couldn't be more different from our 44th President, Barack Hussein Obama. In 2008, I voted for Obama. It was the first time I was able to vote since I turned 18 in 2006. When he was elected, for the first time in my life I was so proud of my country. We elected the first Black president of the United States of America! He was the liberal, well-spoken, intelligent, charismatic, diplomatic, humble, personable, and levelheaded President that we needed after eight years of dealing with George "Dubya" Bush. I voted for Obama again in 2012.

I wasn't used to being proud of my country. It was a really nice feeling that I wasn't very familiar with. Since I had grown up in the midst of George W. Bush's travesty of a presidency, I knew it reflected poorly on me when I told foreigners that I'm from the USA. I was often embarrassed by it. Being able to say, "I'm from the U.S.," without cringing or expecting blowback was a big relief.

Obama did so much good when he was in office. He started to deal with the Great Recession by passing the American Recovery and Reinvestment Act, he made healthcare affordable for millions of people and families, he repealed "Don't Ask, Don't Tell", he made June National Pride Month (this is one of my personal favorites because my birthday is in June), and so much more. He tried to do so much more but a Republican Senate would vote his proposals down every time. I'm honestly surprised that he got as much done as he did. But he was a strong fighter. He was either loved or hated. The latter especially by old, rich, white men.

I was naive to think that because we had a Black President it meant that America wasn't racist anymore. That couldn't be further from the truth. Now the racist white men are less afraid of expressing themselves because there was a Black man in the ultimate position of power and that was too much for their huge white egos to handle. The current President saw the potential of this hate to yield him lots of power and ran with it. That is why we now have children being pulled away from their parents only to be put in cages to die. That is why individuals who are trans are legally being fired because they are trans. That is why the visas of the same sex partners of unmarried United States diplomats and UN employees are being denied.

I haven't even begun to talk about gun control. What's the point? That seems to be the general consensus. I'm not trying to say that Americans don't care about or want gun control. Very many of us do but it doesn't seem to matter or do any good. Politics and money seem to be the only things that matter when it comes to anything of importance for our country and the world.

I'm writing this on September 4th, 2019. We've had a couple of natural disasters as of late that have brought global warming and climate change to the forefront of politics: the first being that the rainforest is on fire and the second is Hurricane Dorian - a slow moving category 5 storm producing winds up to 120 mile an hour. Dorian tied the record for the most powerful Atlantic hurricane ever to come ashore in the Bahamas, equaling the Labor Day hurricane of 1935, before storms were named.

There's a reason for the intensity of Hurricane Dorian and it's called Global Warming. Because of these recent disasters I'm hoping that people are starting to realize that if we don't do something to help our planet, we won't be around much longer to enjoy it. Even if there is numerical data stating that if we don't act soon on climate change, our planet will wipe humanity off of the Earth, we will find some excuse to disregard it.

If somehow we do manage to save the planet, we must save ourselves next and I can only see us doing that with Universal Healthcare, Medicare For All, or some other type of single payer (the government) program, because we can and definitely will keep our Social Security, Medicare, and Medicaid. Too many people's lives depend on these "social" programs for them to be destroyed. Unfortunately, that won't keep the politicians from making devastating cuts.

I learned that firsthand on June 26th, 2018 when my nursing company at the time informed me that PDN (Private Duty Nursing, the sector of North Carolina Medicaid that handles in-home care) was decreasing my nursing hours from 112 a week to 70 hours a week. As was my right, I immediately appealed the decision, but the nightmare had just begun, and it was far from over. For three months I went back and forth between my lawyer from Legal Aid (I am so grateful for this organization!) to the State's Attorney from Medicaid defending my case. It did not matter how many different doctors, respiratory therapists, or nurses wrote and sent in letters stating that I need 24-hour care and supervision. All the state cared about is that I have an able-bodied caregiver who is unemployed living with me.

According to their rules, I was not eligible for more than 76 hours a week. But that low a number would for sure have put a terrible strain on Sean and my relationship and I would have had to choose between whether I wanted to keep my night nursing hours or my day hours, as I would not be able to have both. I knew what the loss of an entire shift could potentially do to Sean's and my life, and it scared the shit out of me! So I argued, I strategized, and I fought to present my case to the best of my ability. The longer the appeal process continued the more likely it seemed that I was not going to receive the ruling I wanted. Therefore, with the help of my nurses we came up with a minimal yet feasible number of nursing hours that we thought would work for my life. I made an offer to the state of 90 hours, to which the state agreed. We were all very relieved that the arduous appeal process was over; unfortunately, the difficult times had just begun.

With the new allotment of hours my nurses are working seven-hour shifts which are shorter than they are used to and therefore they are taking significant pay cuts. Due to their unique sense of loyalty they are sticking with me so far, but we all know and have discussed that it won't be enough to keep them here forever.

Because a seven-hour shift is such an abnormal number of shift hours it's going to be hard to fill them when one of my nurses reaches her limit and decides that she needs to find work elsewhere. Right now, I find myself going without a night nurse voluntarily on the weekend so that my night nurse can pick up the extra hours because I know what she is sacrificing by being here. Although the strain on my relationship with Sean isn't as bad as it would be if my hours had been reduced to 76, my long friendships with some of the people I care about the most, including Sean and the nurses I've had for so long, are definitely being affected by the stress.

These kinds of ridiculous cuts, the high cost of medications, and the fact that single parents are having to work two jobs in order to afford health insurance for their kids, are just a few reasons why the idea of Universal Healthcare is more prevalent today than ever.

Hopefully the next President will fix the dumpster fire of a mess we're in today. Whoever that person is, they have one hell of a job cut out for themselves. I know I don't want that job.

Politics

I love Obama
He's the coolest president
I wish he could stay

Politics

Use your voice and vote
No matter what you believe
Your opinion counts

Politics

COVID-19 spreads
Quicker than the common cold
We saw this coming

Politics

Healthcare is vital
An unhealthy caregiver
Defeats their purpose

Politics

I hate my asshole
It doesn't work properly
I shall call it Trump

Chapter Twelve: Life Stories

While these following haikus could not be categorized among any of the other chapters, it doesn't make them any less important or meaningful than the rest. In fact, some of them are my most important, powerful, and meaningful poems. They either represent an important part of me, my life, or simultaneously something I really wanted to express to others.

Life Stories

Judy is a punk

I want to be sedated

Rock n' roll high school

Life Stories

Sullen Pariah

The pretty goth girl next door

My rad big sister

Life Stories

Pull out couches suck.

They just aren't worth the money

Invest in leather

Life Stories

Call your mama soon.

Haven't talked to her today.

What is up with that?

Life Stories

When you find yourself

In a police state, it's best

Not to ask questions

Life Stories

Our monster mama

She loves us more than herself

She is devoted.

Life Stories

Weird is where it's at

Being "normal" is stranger

Than being bizarre

Life Stories

Beautiful Indy

Much sweeter than red velvet

My fav'rite cupcake

Life Stories

Come get your geek on!

Everyone is welcome here

Geeksboro is home

Life Stories

I'm very lucky

'Cause I can feel everything.

I love affection.

Life Stories

The little red thread

That came out of my cat's butt

Where did he get it?

Life Stories

Jelly suicide

She's her own unique flavor

It tastes great on toast.

Life Stories

Legend of the ring

He's devoted to his craft

His name is Mankind.

www.ingramcontent.com/pod-product-compliance
Lightning Source LLC
Chambersburg PA
CBHW072022060426
42449CB00033B/1654